Orreight mi ol'

(a Sheffield greeting: "Are you all right, my old [love]?")

Observations on dialect, humour and local lore of Sheffield & district

By Don Alexander

Cartoons by Steve Dinsdale (Mono)

Printed by ALD, Sheffield

Printed and published by:

ALD Design & Print

279 Sharrow Vale Road

Sheffield S11 8ZF

Telephone 0114 267 9402

E.Mail a.lofthouse@btinternet.com

ISBN 1-901587-18-5

Copyright Don Alexander 2001

First Published November 2001

Second Edition July 2002

"God must have been a Sheffielder - look at all that theein' an' thouin' in' Bible" - Bobby Knutt

Contents:

Acknowledgements

Don sends his thanks to:

His daughter, Susan, for deciphering his scrawl and typing the book.

His wife, Mary, for her support, the Granelli's sketch and her suggestion for the title 'Orreight mi 'ol'.

Steve Dinsdale, (Mono), for the cartoons done at a time when he was under great personal stress.

Alistair Lofthouse and his team, for taking the risk printing and publishing this book and setting it out so attractively.

Foreword

As an incomer, the South Yorkshire dialect holds a particular fascination for me, because it is a constant reminder of the local industrial and social history of this area. Before I knew Don I was already collecting local words and sayings, so I was flattered to be asked to write this foreword.

There is of course a big difference between the spoken and written word. Both present difficulties for me! On the amateur stage, as Lindley in the Stirrings, I have struggled nobly to shape the words in a Sheffield way, to the amusement of fellow actors.

So now I must rise to the challenge of the written word, by way of the short narrative that follows:

"I went out on 'new bike and it siled it dahn. Weather wor Baltic. When I got 'ome I wor black bright and our mam gid me a good scutching an' sent me ter bed early".

With the help of Don's excellent pocket guide, you can make an accurate translation of the above into the Queen's English. But it won't sound half as colourful!

Paul Iseard

Chapter One - General Comments on Language

Language is always in a state of flux and development - otherwise much of Europe would still be speaking Latin. And, unfortunately for intellectuals like me, thee and us two, the language of the common people usually wins through. For instance, the slang word the vulgar Roman soldiery used for head was *testa*, meaning plant pot, and this became the respectable French word *tête*...... Imagine the Roman troops playing football against the Gauls with a pig's bladder as a ball: *"Get thi plant pot on this, Julius mi ol'"* (my translation).

After the Norman invasion in 1066 the infant English language used basic Anglo-Saxon words alongside ruling-class Norman French, e.g. animals' names were rough and ready Anglo-Saxon whilst their meat became posh Norman French:

Animal	Meat	
Ox	Beef	(French *boeuf*)
Pig	Pork	(French *porc*)
Sheep	Mutton	(French *mouton*)
Calf	Veal	(French *veau*)

The delightful, fresh, almost childlike English of Chaucer (*'wan that Aprile with its shoores soote...'*, *'smalle fowles maken melodye...'*) led to the magnificent language of Shakespeare and the King James (*'Dread Sovereign'*) Bible.

And where does Sheffield English fit into the grand scheme of things, you may ask. Well, it seems to me that our dialect, with its familiar form of address (*thee* and *thou*) is nearer Chaucer and Shakespeare's English than is the current Queen's English. Phrases like *'stint thy clappe'* (Chaucer - meaning *'shut thi trap'*) - and *'what's the matter with thee now?'* (Shakespeare) are pure Sheffield.

In 18th and 19th century literature you can come across words and phrases which were once common but are now possibly confined to our area:
'poor beastie, thou maun live!' (Sheffield *tha mun* = you must) (Robert Burns)

'feeling off the hooks' (Sheffield *'feeling off 'hooks'*, or poorly) (Dickens)

It's as though the powerful tide that is the English language has gone out, leaving discarded remnants in the folds of the Pennine hills (poetic, eh?) We can console ourselves, though, that we're better linguists than the rest of the country, at least when it comes to Northern European languages. Our vowels are pure, like German and Dutch, and the *dee-dah* Sheffielder feels at home when a German says *'dein'* (*thine*) or *'na denn'* (*nah den,* or now then), or a Dutchman says *'t'oud huis'* (*t'owd house*).

In this little book I'm relying on my memory from the 1940s to 2001 of listening to Sheffield people at 'skoyal' - Hillfoot County, Neepsend, then Firth Park Grammar; at 'Lane and Owlerton (Bramall Lane and Hillsborough); on the streets; in pubs and on trams and buses; to Barnsley lads at the KOYLI Barracks in Pontefract in 1959-60; to Rotherhamites from 1961 to 1983 at Park Gate Iron and Steel, then the Ickles, then Brinsworth Strip Mills - also during Saturday work selling Sheffield-made goods at the Rotherham market; and from 1983 to 2001 to all 'sooarts' o' 'fooak' (folk) in my shop on Ecclesall 'Rooad', and in local factories. It's mainly about language but with some remembered local lore. I might have got some things wrong - but I think I'm 'reight'! I must have missed some words and phrases out - please let me know. I've acknowledged other parts of the country - even Leeds - where words and phrases are shared. If you want to do further research , listen to Radio Sheffield - a good confirmation of our dialect - and read 'The Star' and 'The Sheffield Telegraph' where you can find words like *jennel, mardy* and *nesh.* Peter Harvey's articles on *nesh* and *feeling badly* are little jewels. The student should also visit the Centre for English Cultural Tradition and Language at the University of Sheffield, under Professor J.D.A. Widdowson.

Good books to read are:

Sheffieldish by Derek Whomersley, illustrated by Whitworth
(Northends - City of Sheffield Publicity Dept., 1981)

A Glossary of Old Sheffield Trade Words and Dialect by Ronald Dyson, illustrated by J.B. Himsworth
(Sheffield Trades Historical Society, 1936 - reprinted 1979)

The Hallamshire Glossary by Rev. Joseph Hunter. Written 1828 and reprinted with an Introduction by J.A. Widdowson and P.S. Smith in 1983 (The Centre for English Cultural Tradition and Language, University of Sheffield; The Hunter Archaeological Society, Sheffield)

Chapter Two - Theeing and Thouing

My mother didn't like people 'theeing and thouing'. It was for her the thin end of the wedge - talk like that and you were likely to end up 'effin' and blindin' '! Her father, George Hopkinson, was from Matlock. She said he addressed everyone as *'Surrey'*. George came to Sheffield in the early 1900s to work as a grinder on Hollis Croft. They lived in the Philadelphia area of Sheffield (near the Kelvin) and my mother took her father his dinner before going to school, and then she got the cane at school for being late! (no messin' in them days!) He walked everywhere - never took the tram. His wife, my mother's stepmother, was a real Sheffielder and told him *"George, tha'll dee wi' thi booits on"* (he did - dropped dead in Fitzalan Square in 1936).

My father didn't thee and thou either. (Not at home, anyway - perhaps he did at work). He was a military man whose grandfather, John Alexander, came from Empingham in Rutland in the 1890s to work at the huge Vickers steelworks in Sheffield after his 400 acre farm suffered a bad season, forcing him to sell up. My father, like his father before him, joined the Army as a boy and spent many years in India before he was involved in the Second World War. His speech was peppered with Hindi words such as *pawnee* (water), *cup o' cha* (tea) and *look jilde* (get a move on), plus a few British Army French phrases such as *San Fairy Ann (ça ne fait rien,* 'it doesn't matter'*)*, from the Second World War. The only Sheffieldisms I remember were when he drew the curtains together every evening and said *"It wain't get no lighter"*, when he talked about working *'7 while 5'*, and when he used the phrase *'not wiart'* for unless.

With this background my sister, Mary, and myself didn't use the familiar form of address when we started at Hillfoot County School by the River Don at Neepsend in the early 1940s. Right from the start though it interested me why the school teachers spoke differently from their pupils and the people in the street. Being, pardon the Sheffieldism, a 'shrewd little chuff', I thought perhaps they put it on to set themselves apart and make us kids behave ourselves. Of course, no child would address a teacher as *'thee'* - it would have been the end of civilisation as we knew it - but among ourselves there were those who:

1.   like me, could hardly bring themselves to use *'thee'* and *'thou'*;

2.   used *'thee'* and *'thou'* when speaking with children, but not with adults - unless being very rude;

3.   as above, but they pronounced it *'dee'* and *'dah'*. I can't recall utter poverty, but these *'dee-dahs'* tended to be poorer, with torn clothing, holes in their boots, candles hanging from their *nooases* (noses), and if you were eating an apple they would swarm around you shouting *"Save us 'core! Save us 'core!"*

The 'dee-dahs' are unique to Sheffield - so much so that people in Barnsley, Rotherham, Dronfield and Chesterfield call Sheffielders *'dee-dahs'*. (Our Rachel, on a nursing course in Wath-on-Dearne, gets called a *'dee-dah'*). You could call *'dee-dahs'* lazy, or you could say they are more advanced linguistically. Language, like water, takes the easy way and *'dee'* and *'dah'* requires less effort to say than *'thee'* and *'thou'*. (Notice that in saying *'thee'* and *'thou'* the tip of the tongue moves to the back of the front upper teeth. In saying *'dee'* and *'dah'* the tip of the tongue merely touches the front of the upper palate.)

Among adults, theeing and thouing was (and is) common in the workplace - part of the everyday banter and especially in the jollity of *'gooinooam'* time - as any boy squashed between Bassetts Liquorice Allsorts girls or Batchelors *Peyse* (Peas) girls in the back bay of a tram from Wadsley Bridge to Neepsend can testify. I can't recall any woman deeing and dahing, but theeing and thouing was quite common. - though more girls than boys tried to 'speak nice'. One vignette sticks in my memory. When we were about eight, a girl who had just met my mother said *"In't thi mother little?"* and then perhaps sensing I was a bit hurt at this comment, said *"she's better than nowt though, in't she, Donald!"*

In 'A South Yorkshire Family of Type Founders' by William Greaves Blake, William Thompson of Rawmarsh, speaking to his grandson, addresses him using *thou/thee/*

thy (affection). The grandson replies using *you* (respect). Brothers speaking to each other in the same book use *thee/thou/thy* (familiarity). So *thee, thou, thy* and *thine* are simply the familiar or affectionate form of address used in pubs, streets, schools and workplaces exactly like the *tu* form in French and Spanish and *du* in German. The French have a word for it: *tutoyer* (to thee and thou). One difference: our French teacher Dr Eker ('Joe Plug') at Firth Park Grammar School explained how magical it was for a young man or woman when their girl or boy friend started using the familiar form *tu* rather than *vous* - it was the first sign of young love. (It might not be quite the same if a Sheffield lad started addressing his girlfriend as *thee*!) So it was all the more surprising to me when I went to Paris as a callow fifteen year old to stay with my pen pal, Michel, to find everyone addressing each other (and me) as *tu*. The highlight was when his cousin Françoise presented herself in front of me in her bikini, did a Marilyn Monroe wiggle and said *"Donal', tu penses que je suis sexy?"* Steady on, lad, steady on.

Dave D of Hunters Bar has reminded me (March 2002) of the father's warning to his son who's showing a lack of respect:

"Don't thee 'thee-thou' me. Thee 'thee-thou' thissen!"

Once when this followed a list of the boy's faults, including being late for school, the boy replied:

"Way - it's thee-thou-thissen what's made me late for skoyal!"

True Sheffielders are always grammatically correct when they thee and thou. When outsiders 'go native' and imitate us they often get it wrong. Examples of this are:

1. A headline in Sheffield History Reporter, Aug/Sept. 2000: *'Get thee booits on'* (should be *thi* (=thy) not *thee*)

2. A Sunday Times article on Sheffield about 40 years ago. This was quite an endearing article. It's still lodged in my brain and it's still in our loft somewhere. The writer said Sheffielders are hard-faced but easy going. The

city has a worldwide reputation for the quality of its metal goods but retains a market town atmosphere. He went on to say he'd been to a Roses cricket match at Bramall Lane and one man, politely applauding both sides, drew the scorn of a Sheffielder next to him who said:

"Are thee Yorkshire?"
"No."
"Are thee Lancashire?"
"No."
"Then mind own bloody business."
The Sheffielder, of course, would say *a'tha* (*art thou*) and *mind **thi** own business.*

The use of *thee, thou, thy, thine* is not peculiar to Sheffield, of course. It is found across a wide swathe of the North and Midlands, in Devonshire I believe, and even in the USA, but it is especially prevalent in the Steel City and towns in a ring around Sheffield: Penistone, Barnsley, Mexborough, Rotherham, Doncaster, Worksop, Chesterfield, Dronfield, Mansfield, and .... Abney Low, Derbyshire. (A Derbyshire bloke told me that at this settlement 1100 feet high in the Peak District, near enough to *Sheffel'* - as he called it - to thee and thou, there's a farm called 'Cockeye Farm', named after two cock-eyed men who bumped into each other. One said: *"Ah wish tha'd look weer tha'rt gooing"* and the other replied *"ah wish tha'd go weer tha'rt looking!"*)

A little practice: *'Ear all, see all, say nowt*
               Eight* all, sup all, pay nowt
               *eat is pronounced eight
               An' if tha ever does owt fer nowt
               Allus do it fer thissen.

And: *What's thine's mine and what's mine's mi own.*

Chapter Three - The Sheffield Glottal Stop

Everyone can mimic the Cockney mid-word glottal stop. This is the replacement of the 't' sound in the middle of a word by a brief stoppage of the air passage by the back of the tongue. (The missing 't' is represented by an apostrophe: *wa'er, be'er, bu'er*. Imagine Peggy Mitchell in 'East Enders' speaking to Frank Butcher:

"Fwank, this beer taists like wa'er - and while you're there doing nofink you'd be'er bwing some bu'er fwom the fwidge." Easy!

The Sheffield glottal stop, by contrast, is hard to describe and even harder for outsiders to master. It is the virtual disappearance of the definite article, the word *'the'*. If you're long in the tooth like me and remember the Danish comedian Victor Borge you will recall that Danes tend to pronounce the English 'the' with their tongues right out beyond their lips, as if they're being rude. With some Lancastrians 'the' is shortened to *'th'* - tongue just between the teeth - as in *'Th'Irlam o' th'heights'*. When I lived in Manchester a lad from Bacup used to talk about *'putting a bun in th'oven'*. Recently (8th July 2001) Rita in Coronation St. ('Coro') said *"I've sent Norris to th'wholesalers"*). In the West Riding 'the' has merely become a 't', as it perhaps was once in Sheffield: *'T'Wicker weer t'watter runs o'er t'weer'* (The Wicker where the water runs over the weir). Again, Sheffielders have advanced linguistically (or become lazier in their speech) and 'the' has become the briefest of stoppages of the air passage by the tip of the tongue. This is indicated by an apostrophe. So *'in the water'* becomes:
in th'watter in Lancashire
in t'watter in the West Riding
in 'watter in Sheffield and district.

Outsiders and actors almost invariably have trouble with the Sheffield glottal stop - listen to Robert Carlyle's otherwise credible attempt at a local accent in 'The Full Monty'. In Kay Mellor's 'Fat Friends' (TV play, late 2000) a character says *"Kevin set fire to shop"*. Getting it wrong like this, missing out the definite article altogether - not even giving it the decency of a glottal stop - sounds dead ignorant to me.

Finally, here's a classic example of the Sheffielder's humour and his glottal stop:

A cricket match at Bramall Lane between Yorkshire and South Africa was taking its tedious course when a black dog ran on the pitch. The players tried to catch it and a policeman dived and missed before it eventually ran off the field. Play continued tediously as before and after a few minutes a wag in the crowd yelled *"Send 'dog back on ageean!"*

Chapter Four - Skoyal

In the 1940s infants of five years old were taken by their mothers to school on their first day or two. Thereafter they went on their own or with older children. If they cried and still needed their 'mam' they were likely to be classed as *'mardy'*. Children would chant

"Mardy bum, mardy bum
Tell your mother to smack your bum"

I was a dreamer. My friend Alan Cottingham was also a dreamer. The walk from Parkwood Road to Hillfoot County School should have taken 15 minutes - it took us well over half an hour:

- The ruins at the bottom of Parkwood Road (where houses had been 'blitzed' beyond repair) had to be examined. We convinced ourselves there was the smell of *'deead'* bodies;

- Ears had to be pressed against tramway poles to catch the hum of a distant tram car;

- The crimped steel bottle tops at the vinegar factory had to be collected and skimmed across the road;

- And most important, most hypnotic, the men rolling steel at Andrew's Toledo's wire rod mill had to be watched. Pairs of shining steel rolls, with grooves in them, all revolving at high speed, were set side by side across the middle of the mill floor. The floor was made of steel plates, made shiny by men's boots and hot steel rod whipping and snaking over it at speed. The process started with a steel billet, perhaps 3 in. square by 6 ft. long, being drawn from the reheating furnace, glowing hot, ready for rolling. There were perhaps four men, two each side of the rolls, moving as gracefully as in a ballet, catching the hot steel with their tongs and passing it through the series of rolls, the billet being reduced to rod and getting longer and longer as it moved faster and faster until, going through the final set of rolls at its fastest, it was caught by the end man who ran with it to the coiling machine. In the meantime, the first men of the team were already rolling down the next billet... *"Shall we just watch one more?"* ..Then another!…It was fascinating - The men's shouts, whistles and songs, echoed to the girders of the huge black shed as we watched silently through the big gates of the loading bay.

Our idyllic progress was brutally halted one day when we were looking over Hillfoot Bridge at the River Don flowing fast after heavy rain. A gang of school bullies got hold of us - one thumped me on the nose (*"ah gorrim reight on 'nooase"*, he said triumphantly. It was a big enough target even then!) Worse, they then held us by our ankles over the river. *"Don't worry, Donald"*, Alan said, his face upside down next to mine. *"They daren't drop us."* Not dialect, this, but just to give you a flavour of life in old Neepsend.

ah gorrim reight on 'nooase

A verbal threat to naughty young lads at the time was *" 'Bobby'll 'ave yer"*. The only time we had a brush with the law as I remember - apart from once when we were caught exploring 'The Ruins' with Tom Slaney - was playing football with the mill blokes on our road. We were about ten years old. The blokes played in their steel capped, steel studded clogs, and there were no concessions to us young 'uns when they did sliding tackles, a stream of sparks issuing from the contact of boots to cobbles.

"Have a heart, constable", one said, *"we get our punishment climbin' o'er 'gasworks wall when we loise 'ball o'er theer."*

(What did he mean, **we**? - They pushed us young 'uns over the high wall to look for the ball among big steel pipes reeking of gas.)

What else do I remember of dialect in those distant Infant and Junior school days by the Don? ....Mainly obscenities, I much regret to say. Why is it we remember things that are not worth remembering and forget things that are? Anyway, stop faffin' around, Donald. Publish and be damned:

Insult: *"Shut thi gob - an' gi' thi arse a chance"* (Even my sister Mary, normally polite and well spoken, was provoked into saying this now and again.)

Another insult (to someone who is dithering, can't make up his mind when faced with many choices)**:** *"Tha'rt like a fart in a culinder - can't gerraht fer 'oils"* (can't get out for holes)
This I thought was pure Sheffield (or rather 'impure' Sheffield) but a Glaswegian used it in a TV series about British builders in Spain. I've forgotten what it was called - the one with Jimmy Nail...

Verse: *'Me, thee and us two met a merry lass...*

I must draw a veil over this one……. should I just say the last word on each of the subsequent lines is:

grass
clothes
tha knows!

About somebody mean: *"He wain't part wi' 'snot from 'is nooase"*

A jolly little rude rhyme: *'One day down at Brammer Lane*
    We were playing at cricket
    'Ball went up mi trouser leg
    An' hit mi middle wicket'

Going to Firth Park Grammar a few years later with Alan and his brother Eric we took the tram to the bottom of Herries Road near the Wednesday ground, then the bus to the school. At some point in the journey Eric would say *"Skoyal ageean. Skoyal ageean"*. What a depressing thought! In those days - early 1950s - dialect was less acceptable than it is today and to 'get on' it was deemed necessary to put on a BBC accent! In the lower 6th Gerald Brooke decided to use the southern long 'a' and altered his speech almost overnight. A few years later Gerald was the cause of national concern when he was held in Lubianka KGB Gaol in Moscow. We can't blame his 'southern' accent for that, though.

I was hesitant in my speech - I couldn't talk posh, neither could I use dialect, but dialect interested me and I have a keen memory of it. (See chapter 11 for the list of Sheffield expressions passed around Sheffield schools at the time).

At Neepsend even university was regarded as *'skoyal'*. Back in Sheffield after my first term in Manchester in 1956, a woman from the top of Parkwood Rd greeted me: *"Still skoyalin' Donald? Our George's earnin' £10 a week down 'pit."* The pit was a ganister drift mine that went into the big hill that is Parkwood Springs. (There's a ski slope near there now - who'd have thought it?) Ganister, or 'gani', is a grey refractory silicious rock once used in the iron and steel industry for, e.g. plugging the blast furnaces at Park Gate, Rotherham. My brother-in-law, Cyril Boswell, worked in this mine and has funny stories of following a seam and emerging among the allotments and surprised allotment holders on Parkwood Springs. Not so funny was the danger of silicosis - *"When tha gets that th'art booked fer a pair o' wings",* he used to say. Now he's got it, but hopefully won't get his wings for many years yet.

Chapter Five - Football
(in the street, or down at 'Lane or Owlerton (Bramall Lane or Hillsborough)

My mother was only small but she was determined. She got me and some other Neepsend lads to join the Life Boys, and later the Boys Brigade at Victoria Hall Methodist Church in Norfolk St. Religious zeal spread like wildfire across Penistone Road, across the Don, around Farfield Road and Parkwood Road, and up Parkwood Springs. 'Onward Christian Soldiers' was never sung so aggressively. My sister and other Neepsend girls joined the Girls Life Brigade……..But was it religious zeal, in the boys' case, or the football teams you could get into? We shall never know.

Playing with the steelworkers had made us quick and agile and - dare I say it - a bit rough. Victories of up to twenty-nowt were rung through to the 'Green Un'. Other Sheffield *'teeams'* had no chance against us. (That'll stir things up among some of you lot reading this!) Our 'home' ground was up at Worrall, on a slope like a lot of Sheffield pitches. Once it was so windy we found the wooden changing hut had blown down the hill.

Most of our class at Hillfoot were Wednesdayites - on one famous occasion Wednesday played Doncaster Rovers in the 'County Cup' final at Hillsborough. It was a mid-week match. There were <u>52 000</u> spectators including most of the lads and a few lasses from our class.

Next day all the lads who'd wagged *'skoyal'* lined up to be caned. I wasn't among them because I was a Unitedite (*"An' then tha wonders why tha never had any friends"* says my brother-in-law Cyril, a true-blue Wednesdayite).

My father, in the few years I knew him, took me, our Mary, Sheila Crookes and Iris Spencer *ter' Lane* to see some real football players like Jimmy Hagan - a man of immense skill. Not 'kick and rush' like at Hillsborough. (My father later had an arrangement to go with his son-in-law Cyril *ter 'Lane* one week, *'ter Owlerton* the next. He kept his bargain for the *Lane* matches but never went to Hillsborough!) Wednesdayites, in contrast, saw United as a *'one man teeam'* and sang to the tune of 'Covered Wagon':

Roll along, Sheffield United, roll along
To the bottom of the league where you belong
If Hagan gets the ball he's sure to slip and fall
Roll along, Sheffield United, roll along

Alternatively they'd sing about their own team (*'..to the top of the league..'*, *'..if Quigley* [later Dooley] *gets the ball he's sure to score a goal..'* etc.). Unitedites, of course, sang their own version.....All innocent stuff.

I ramble on a lot now, as is my wont (or should it be 'as is my *waint*', in Sheffield dialect?) In those days, however, I saw and heard all and said nowt. I never showed much emotion - even when Jimmy Hagan scored a beauty. My dad said I'd make a good spy.

I liked to watch the reaction of the crowd as well as watch the play on the field. Bramall Lane covered a huge area with football pitch and cricket pitch side by side . On match days half time and full time scores for all the other teams in the league were hung up under the cricket pavilion in big white-on-black numbers. Wednesday's match score was hung up every fifteen minutes.

Once with Wednesday's score 0-0 the scoreboard man walked slowly towards Wednesday's slots - carrying a number 6 and another hidden number behind it. Immense excitement, unbearable anticipation. *"Wednesday's loisin' 6-nowt"* said the optimist. *"Or winnin' 6-nowt"* put in the pessimist. The scoreboard man then turned the 6 round to reveal a 1 on the other side and hung it with the other number - also a 1.

Sometimes when Wednesday were *'loisin'* the cheer would be so great that United's opponents would stop in bewilderment on the field wondering what was happening!

…Any rooad up don't forget - 'football is a game of two *aives*' (Dunt he say some daft things!)

Chapter Six - Places in and around Sheffield

Sheffield rises from about two hundred feet above sea-level in the East End at Attercliffe right up to a thousand feet and above at the extreme West. The moors rise to fifteen hundred feet at High Neb on Stanage Edge.

Areas reflect this topography:

She lives	*up Worrall*
	up Walkley
	up Crookes
	up Gleadless
	up Fulwood
	up Norton
	up Lodge Moor
	up Rivelin
	down Neepsend
	down Attercliffe (or *on 'Cliff*)
He works	*down 'East End*
	down Rotherham way
	at Firths (Firth Brown)
	at Metros (Metropolitan Vickers)
	at Ooslams or *Oosnams* (Wostenholms)
	at Sammy Osborns
	at Steelos (Steel Peech and Tozer)
	at 'Fooage (Park Gate Iron and Steel)
	in 'rollin' mills
	in 'coggin' mill
	on 'hammers
	on 'furnaces

Once when I was going to work at Heeley Sidings I stood on a tram stop 'island' at the end of Nursery St. at about half past five in the morning, waiting for a tram. I got talking to a Mancunian. We were going against the tide - a huge wave of silent men with a scattering of women walking - on bikes - in cars - on trams and buses funnelling through the Wicker Arches into the East End with its wall-to-wall steel and engineering works covering the lower Don Valley to Rotherham and beyond. The Mancunian said he'd never seen such a busy city at such an early hour and I felt an immense pride in this city and these men.

I had another holiday job as a schoolboy cutting the hedges with hand shears in the 1950s working for Sheffield Corporation Parks Department around Graves Trust homes scattered around the city. It was with an interesting team - a Ukrainian fascist who had fought with the German Army against the Russians, a boy called David who at snap - time drooled over the women in the 'Reveille' newspaper. Finally there was a small, wizened old bloke whose name I forget. He was the most interesting of the three - a real old Sheffielder - or, may I say, *Sheffelder*.

David thrust a 'Reveille' pin-up under his nose - a big, curvy girl with a big toothy smile. *"David"*, he said, *"tha cudn't keep her in toothpaste"*. David said to get money he'd *"goo in 'works down 'East End"*, but did the old man know what it was like working *"dahn theer"*? He replied *"It's no good asking me David. I'm lost when I'm past 'Wicker Arches!"*

That reminds me: there's a saying 'to have a grin as wide as 'Wicker Arches', and 'to have a face as long as Norfolk Street'. And the Sheffield University rag magazine was called TWIKKER. It maybe still is.

Most of you will know the Sheffield curse *'flippin' Heeley'* and are probably aware that the Meers Brook was the Derbyshire/Yorkshire boundary, but have you heard of *Heeley duffers*? These were criminals who lived just over the boundary in Derbyshire - committed their dirty deeds in Sheffield then scarpered off home to avoid capture.

This courtesy of Lynda Taylor who lived as a child at 'the top of Heely Bottom'. A lad who played ball with her use to cry "cob it o'er 'wire" = chuck it over the lone telephone wire.

Derbyshire and the Peak District is the first love for many Sheffielders, but despite this we have the saying:

Derbyshire born
Derbyshire bred
Strong in 'arm
Weak in 'ed.

(Derbyshire people say it should be *wick,* meaning clever - not weak).

The rhyme is said in Manchester about Cheshire people, and Ken Dodd says it about Yorkshire people - adding *"Are there any Yorkshiremen in the audience? Ah, there they are, clustered around the exit - in case there's a collection!"*

Chapter Seven - Military Interlude

Please translate: *"Ah'm excused booits and laikin' so ahm liggin' in me own pog in' barricks"* Clue: he's a Barnsley lad.

For Sheffielders the military medical centre for National Service men in the 1950s was in offices above Hartley's potted meat factory on Ecclesall Road (right above where the 'Don Alexander' Sheffield Shop is now).

I passed for the R.A.F. but they kept me waiting for weeks and, being a bit of a rebel in those days, I sent them a nasty letter saying I didn't want to join the Airforce, but seeing as I'd got to, get me in now and let me get it over with. I was half hoping they'd refuse to have me. I was half right - they didn't want me …… they let the Army sort this bolshy chappie out.

So on Bonfire night 1959 I had to report to the Light Infantry Barracks at Pontefract - Inkermann platoon KOYLI and DLI lads from Barnsley, Wakefield, Halifax, Sunderland, Newcastle, Durham. Marching pace - one hundred and eighty steps a minute; drill; five mile runs; drill; route marches; drill; PE; drill; weapon training in fast and harassing, intimidating sequence. Initiative test on North York Moors - to avoid capture by military and civil police. I used my initiative, hitched to Leeds for a weekend with my future wife Mary.

The Sunderland DLI lad I was teamed with to clean the kitchens and peel spuds as a punishment said the army got worse potatoes than he'd had in Durham gaol. When we cut out all the bad bits, as an experiment, the potatoes were the size of *peyse* (peas).

"Booits, booits, booits" as a Barnsley, Penistone or Stocksbridge Rudyard Kipling might have said. Hours were spent bulling up same. One advantage: Pickerings of Sheffield 'Blanco' for belts and webbing had become Pickerings of Sheffield light infantry dark green polish. By the way, if you can't get to Barnsley to hear their dialect, listen to Barnsley people phoning Radio Sheffield or being interviewed -

preferably by Tony Capstick. (Tony, with his feature *'Lurv in the afternooin' '* is a real Barnsley lad - well, Mexborough, but that's near enough).

Note that in Barnsley a C&A store would be *'coits an' 'ats'*, whereas in Sheffield it was *'cooats an' 'ats'*. Sometimes it can be something rude but we'll draw a veil over that.

Laikin' means playing. I'm told that it also has the connotation of shirking - miners were often *laikin'* Mondays. (My cousin Byron worked for eight years down Smithy Wood and later Manton collieries rather than do two years military service, and he used to say he'd get that 'Tuesday morning feeling' when starting the week's work. The Sheffield cutlers' excuse for not working Mondays was that it was a Saints Day - 'Saint Monday'. God sent Monday. - Where do I get it all from?

Over to Tony Capstick, Radio Sheffield, 8/9/01. "I'm off till Wednesday but I'm not *laikin'* (=shirking) - well, I am *laikin'* (=playing) as a policeman [in a TV series]".

Liggin' is a fine word, and I don't need to tell you it means 'lying (down)'. This was much used among the Barnsley lads at 'Ponti'. After the exhausting training, *liggin'* in bed was bliss. And it is a venerable word. Chaucer used it in the 1300s: *'and foond thee ligging by his wife'*. (Trust Chaucer to use it cheekily!)

In 'A Glossary of Old Sheffield Trade Words and Dialect', *to lig on* = 'to lay on a great deal of pressure in filing or grinding'.

Pog - one's own bedspace; a seat; if you're going in a pub in Mexborough *"save us a pog"*.

Half way through basic training at Ponti I passed an interview at the War Office for a six month Russian course, which was subject to successful completion of infantry training. Back at Pontefract the Sergeant Major now took to calling me *'effin' Kruschev'*!

26

On the Russian course at the RAEC Barracks, Beaconsfield, me and a Glasgow lad, who was also interested in dialect, formed the *'Liggin' Corps'*. It was the duty of this corps to use every opportunity to *'lig'* on your bed, while chanting out Russian military vocabulary, it must be said. There was a big test every month with the prospect, after completing the course, of joining the Intelligence Corps in civvies at GCHQ, Cheltenham for a while before moving to Berlin. Fail any one test and I'd have been back in the infantry ....

A London lad, posh spoken, ex public school, could only speak Russian with a strong Southern English accent. I ridiculed this and he ridiculed my Northern accent - called me Wilfred Pickles and came out with a string of Northern patois - as he saw it:

"Ey up lad - there's trouble in t'mill - we're not mekkin' enough brass - Jimmy Hardcastle tha'll av to work Christmas day on th'looms for nowt, otherwise I don't rightly know how th'mill'll goo on. I don't rightly know .... It's not champion isn't that".

He was a regular, poor on the rifle range, so when he practised golf in the barracks and said he'd hit Alexander's head I didn't worry because I felt sure he'd miss. I was *'ligging'* down reading 'Pravda' when CLUNK. He was so apologetic. We had become almost friendly, but I was rather pleased when next day, lined up on an extremely hot parade ground, he crumpled to the floor in a faint, rifle clattering onto the sacred square. As he fell the Sergeant Major yelled *"Get a grip of yourself, that man!"* I was reminded of him when idly watching a Perry Mason repeat on television . A Texan in the film drawled *"I don't rightly know"*. Is this pseudo Yorkshire dialect, or American? I don't rightly know.

Chapter Eight - Trade Terms and Trade Humour

We had a holiday in Stresa, Italy a few years ago and I was pleased to see the window of a local jeweller's full of Sheffield silver frames - made at Ron Carr's Holbrook factory. A hand-written cardboard sign read:

'Argenti di Scheffeld'

The Italians had put a teutonic *c* in and had left the *i* out, as we sometimes do in *Sheffel'* itself.

The very word Sheffield is the world's best trade term in itself, signifying quality whether it be steel, knives or silver. Three small examples from visitors to my shop of its world wide significance:

- An American lady driving from London to Edinburgh for a day trip saw the word 'Sheffield' and thought to her surprise that this must be the place where best quality knives were made. She found her way to Ecclesall Road and bought one. She admitted she didn't realise Sheffield was an 'English town'. For her it was just the name on quality knife blades.

- Japanese steelmen from Kobe here to buy our special aerospace steels. One said *"Of course we learn about Sheffield steel in our schools"*.

- An Indian man from a small village near Madras. *"I'd heard so much about Sheffield steel it was almost a religious experience to come here"*.

Solingen, the German cutlery town, has had a special stamp issued by 'Deutsch Postamt' in its honour. Thiers, the French cutlery town, has been similarly honoured by the French Post Office. Has our Post Office ever celebrated Sheffield steel and cutlery? No chance. Muffin the Mule has had more success. So it behoves us to blow our own trumpet loudly - we can't rely on others.

In his 'Glossary of Words and Dialect formerly used in the Sheffield Trades', Ronald Dyson writes:

' Before the days of steam power and the large factories, the work in Sheffield was done in small works or 'wheels' built on one of the five streams: the Don, Sheaf, Rivelin, Loxley or Porter, and each was equipped with one or more water wheels to drive the tiny factory …… the practised eye of these skilled men could judge accurately the correct temperature to harden or 'work' their steel, whilst the tilters, forgers and rollers could hammer and roll their steel into the desired shapes with remarkable skill and judgement. They were cautious of new methods or changes, and almost proud of their conservatism. They did not mix very well with the inhabitants of other towns, for to them Sheffield was the hub of the universe.

Their dialect was full of curious and individual trade terms and in this they showed the same reluctance to change as in other matters. Thus it is that even today, when education has almost destroyed the dialects, the true 'Shevvild' can still be heard in all its richness and purity among the older craftsmen in the local trades. With the transition to machine methods, the further spread of education, and the effect of the wireless, it is unlikely that Sheffield dialect will be able to last out much longer. It will be a foreign language to future generations. '

This was written in 1936 and in 2001 I find that most of the words he lists as 'formerly used in the Sheffield Trades' are **still** used today in the cutlery trade. They are a long time dying! I'll list those which I think will be of interest:

***Arseboard* or *Horseboard*:** a board slung from behind the grinder to serve as a seat. It extends forwards between his legs to the wheel. His weight converts it into a powerful lever for pressing objects to be ground on the stone.

***Bearded*, of a penknife:** Having a very short bolster. (There are unusual names for different bolsters on table knives: *Yankee* bolster, *flush* bolster, and what about this one - *egg waterloo* bolster).

Bolster stone: A narrow grindstone for grinding bolsters and removing fash. There's a nice stone village of this name at the top of Ewden valley with its church and stocks and remains of its glass industry. The fields off More Hall Lane were excellent for blackberries, hence my mother's song:

Bolsterstone, Bolsterstone
Gathering blackberries at Bolsterstone
They are so sweet
And good to eat
(It never became a hit).

Buffing: highly polishing a blade with a leather covered wooden wheel, or buff. Originally the covering was buffalo leather.

Bug blinding: limewashing the workshop. Mr. Ed Chapman of Heeley, pen/pocket knife and scissor grinder working from 1915 to 1972 (he's a hundred this year, I believe) said he didn't like his shop *whiteweshed* - he couldn't see his work so well. I've heard this same complaint recently from workers at A. Wright's who've moved this year from their quaint Sidney Street premises to equally quaint but newly *whiteweshed* premises on Charles Street.

Bull Week: the week before Christmas - overtime worked to pay for the holiday.

Burnt blades: blades overheated on the wheel so that their temper is spoiled.

Burritted heads: rivet heads protruding a little from the handle and finished and polished in the form of a little round cap (Spanish beretta).
Incidentally, **rivets** are pronounced *revits*, **scissors** *sithers*, and **patterns** *pattrens*.
Clout: a cloth used for wiping knives. You'll know dish clout - dishcloth. It was used by women to swipe their male offspring with: *'I'll clout thee one in a minute'*.
An old Hillfoot school carol:
Good King Wenceslas knocked a copper senseless
Outside Marks & Spencers
Copper came out and gave him a clout

And that made Wenceslas senseless.

Cuckoos: faulty work sent back to put right. Ed Chapman talks of giving men 'cuckoo' - greeting them with cries of 'cuckoo' when they were guilty of faulty work. I've also heard it from men in pocket knife workshops to-day.

To hear words like this, thought to be extinct, is as interesting to me as hearing the bird itself up at Strines Moors in May.

Datal: paid by the day - not piecework. Not to be confused with the shiftwork terms *'on days', 'on afters', 'on neets'* (steel and engineering works usually work round the clock).

Dolly: a wheel of calico cloth discs clamped together revolving on a glazer's spindle, used for polishing cutlery etc. (Is the word the source of Sheffield dialect for left handed - *dolly posh*? Probably not. The dolly tub and the wooden posher were, of course, precursors of the washing machine and this is probably the source… .mentioned again later).

Fey: to clean out the sludge or mud from a grinder's *trow* (trough) under his wheel. (German *'fegen'*, to clean). Ed Chapman, the Heeley pocket knife grinder previously mentioned, a hundred years old and brain as sharp as his knives, said when he started work in 1915 he had two *trows* at Ibbersons, Rockingham Lane. With sandstone wheels he had to clean the *trows* out every three months - with *'patent'* wheels (artificial stone) *feying* was done every six months.

Bill Hukin, razor grinder, told me in 1993 that if the wheel was clogged up it was 'snotty'.

Hull: a grinding shop - also a pig sty!

Jimping: milling the edge of a blade.

***Lamb foot/sheep foot* blade:** type of straight tapering blade in a pocket knife.

Little mester: a master cutler working on his own.

Mousing: glazing down of bone, wood, pearl, etc. (derives from unpleasant mouse smell when glazing bone).

Moit: a mote in the eye - steel or stone particle usually. Grinders are experts at removing these.

Outworker: independent cutler 'factoring' - doing work for larger firms.

Pile side: one of my favourites - the side of the blade opposite to that carrying the mark. Reverse side.

Dyson says this is the side where the iron of the tang is piled up on the steel of the blade. But this applied only to shear steel table knife blades and the phrase is used today both for table/dessert knives and pocket/pen knives.
I think the word has the same derivation as the French *'pile ou face'* (heads or tails). I don't think anybody else has pointed this out - so remember, it was me what *fon* this out. (Since writing this I've read 'The Hallamshire Glossary', and Hunter writes *"Mark and Pile are used of a knife, as head and tail of a coin.."* He didn't make the French connection though).

To race: to true up irregularities of wear on a grindstone. *Racin' 'stooan.*

Rammel: Refuse of any kind. Used both at Hillfoot Junior and Firth Park Grammar schools.
I've heard both Rony Robinson and Tony Capstick use the word on Radio Sheffield. Rony was talking about antiques and said of something: *"It's rammel. Chuck it away!"*

Rooak (Roke): surface defect on table knife. Used in steelmaking for defects on the surface of billets, bars, strip etc.

Rozzil: resin - used for fixing tangs of blades into the handle. *Rozziled in.*

Sham pin: a pin or rivet in a knife that does not pass through the tang (for a knife to look better than it is).

Snaith or snath: the crooked handle of a big scythe shaped to the man using the scythe. Sheffield scythe blade manufacturers such as Burgon & Ball, Tyzack and Sorby-Hutton use US ash or now, aluminium *snaths*.

Souring: drawing pay for work not yet done.

Sweets: (the opposite of *sours*) goods delivered but not yet paid for.

Stock: oak tree stump let deep into the ground for the hand-forger's stiddy (small anvil) or stithy (larger anvil). ('Just look at this anvil' translated into Sheffield dialect would be: *'Sithee at this stithy, sithee'*).

When I talked to Jack Hawksworth, owner of J.B. Rawlins Hope Works, Harvey Clough Road, in 1973, he said the bases for the anvils were usually large blocks of sandstone - he called these 'stiddies' (stones with a recess for the anvils to sit in). He used to collect horse muck as a boy in the 1920s to put in these recesses as a kind of shock absorber. He said the horse muck was like dried tinder when used, and it helped to prevent hand forgers getting 'dropped wrist' - repetitive strain or damage to the wrist after years of hammering hot steel.

Takkin' ageean: file maker's equivalent of 'cuckoos' - correcting faulty work. Joe Atkins, who worked at E.S.C., Holme Lane, confirms this.

Tek thi hook: Go quickly!

Thumb mark: the mark on a Shear steel or Double Shear steel Victorian-to-1920s knife where the iron tang has been welded to the steel blade.

Wasters: rejects, seconds. By extension: ne'er do wells!

Whetstone: a slab of Brincliffe blue stone (Brincliffe Edge in Sheffield). The warehouse women swish the knife edge quickly along to make a keen cutting edge.

Bill Hukin, a razor grinder who used to come in our shop, talked about a woman *"who couldn't whet lettuce"*.

Yarmouth beef: in the days when boats followed the shoals of herring (now extinct), 'red herrings' (two-eyed beef steak) were the only 'beef' an impoverished cutler could afford.

Yaller belly: a grinder daubed by yellow swarf from the wheel. Lincolnshire people are also called 'yellow bellies'. A Lincolnshire man at Park Gate Iron and Steel told me why but I can't repeat it.

Some funny memories and anecdotes in Rotherham and Sheffield industry (well, I think they were funny)**:**

Arnold Saxton was an essential member on morning orders meetings at Park Gate Iron and Steel in the 1960s, along with representatives from the melting shop, the rolling mills, Metallurgical and Testing departments, and Sales. Customers' orders were passed around for comments/instructions and were entered for production, acknowledged, and sometimes even rolled the same day. It was a very efficient steel works run with almost religious zeal - the directors were strict Methodists and clocked on and off like everyone else. Arnold had lists of stock ingots rejected for one reason or another - out on analysis usually, and it was his skill to pluck them out of his lists and slot them into any order that was remotely suitable:

"I've got five ingots, cast C5644, out just 0.05 on carbon - alter 'analysis to mek it reight. It'll do 'job. Brummies wain't know 'difference". It was called 'ladling and teeming' - balancing things out.

I once asked him if a certain steel of unusual analysis ordered by a foreign firm could be rolled.

"For thee, Don lad, we'd roll it in Bri-Nylon".

Lads new to the industry might start as 'paint lads', their job being to paint the ends of bars and billets in different colours to distinguish different specifications. One lad ran out of black paint, used his initiative and painted the ends white, and in bold white letters down the billet painted: THIS WHITE PAINT IS BLACK. On a German order stipulating paint mark *schwarz* (black) he carefully painted the word SCHWARZ on the steel - in yellow paint!

Jimmy M., big, bustling Rotherhamite who took problems onto his broad shoulders, came straight out with remarks that I found so funny I logged them down. (Rather as the journalist and author Stephen McClarence wrote about Sheffield's Liverpudlian councillor Moscroft). Unfortunately I gave someone the list and I've not seen it since but Jimmy would say:

"We're still feightin' at Sankeys" (a GKN Midlands customer)

"Nah then Bill - is it six loads at Gate Ten or ten loads at Gate Six?"

Bustling into the 11 inch Continuous Bar Mill on reports of a ghost being sighted on the night shift:

"Nah then, show me what you can't see".

On being told **"you'll** have to do" when customer couldn't contact the sales director or the sales manager:

"He gus reight round 'houses an' ends up wi' rubbin' rag".

Finally, a very rude one that could only come from a Rotherham steelman - on being harassed and frustrated at every turn:

"It's like shittin' in bed awak an' shovin' it out wi' thi feet!"

Awak brings to mind the story of Samuel Fox, one of the great Victorian steelmen - he who invented the folding umbrella frame and whose Fox Paragon umbrellas are still carried by City Gents .... One of his less effective workers reported that a favourite worker of Fox's was asleep.

"Ne'er mind", said Fox, *"he's worth more to me asleep than thou art awak"*.

At Brinsworth Strip Mills we had a Danish customer, a firm named **'Thiis'** (pronounced *tease*) and one day when we'd a transport problem Steve S. came storming in:

"Don, what's all this about this bloody This!"

Our Dutch agent Kees Duvendijk became in Rotherham 'Keith Diving Duck'. If we were late on a delivery Kees would say *"Dish ish terrible. I'm going to throw my shelf in the canal"*.

The big Rotherham bar mills at Aldwarke and Roundwood, Rotherham send a hundred thousand tonnes a year to the USA to manufacturers in cities along the Great Lakes, and a hundred thousand tonnes to Germany to manufacturers in the Ruhr Valley. Re-sulphurised, free cutting, easy machining steels, invented at Park Gate Iron and Steel Co., Rotherham, before the Second World War, with many subsequent refinements, lend themselves to volume production of parts for the motor trade.

The Yanks think big and when Champion Spark Plug at Toledo, Ohio wanted to try our steel they didn't just order a 2 tonnes trial as British firms might do - their sample order was 500 tonnes! Customers in cities such as Detroit/Cleveland/ Buffalo/Chicago wanted monthly supplies around the year and a problem was that the Great Lakes froze over in winter.

Our shipping office solved this by arranging for thousands of tonnes to be shipped in winter to a port near the mouth of the Mississippi, and nine barges, each containing a thousand tonnes of Rotherham steel, were lashed together there and pushed up the Mississippi, then on to the Northern Lakes. Once a barge broke free and sank in the Mississippi, but what an achievement!

An American customer in Detroit asked if we could barge the steel direct from Rotherham, with no handling by dockers. Percy O., our shipping manager, sent him a picture of a 90 tonnes Sheffield and South Yorkshire Navigation barge with the caption *'Do you think this could cross the Atlantic?'*

The Sheffield and South Yorkshire Navigation was widened to admit bigger barges, and I believe a dock at Aldwarke may be constructed to allow 900 tonnes loads to be barged to the Humber, the barge and its load to be lifted on to a 'mother ship' then put down on the Rhine to continue its way to the 'Ruhrgebiet'.

This was tried in the 1970s but it was in the days when the dockers were too powerful and they wouldn't allow 'piggy-backing' barge to ship. As our shipping supremo Mike B. said at the time *"It was only an 'ad-hog' arrangement"*.

Mike was able to solve problems with customers whilst keeping a sense of humour. He could make a joke, some corny, out of every name. When we had trouble with payments from Ahmenabad Advance Mills and further shipments were stopped, he thumped the table and said "Ahm en a bad mood about this!" Again - it seemed funny at the time.

Sheffielder Terry T. was a leading metallurgist at Rotherham works in the 1970s and early 1980s when I was there, and he introduced me to the greeting that is the title of this book: yes, the famous *'ORREIGHT MI OL''*. It is, of course, short for 'Are you all right, my old love', and is usually a man to man greeting. If Terry was in a hurry he'd just greet you with *'mi ol''*. Pure Sheffield - one of my favourite expressions and it's fairly common in buses and in pubs if you keep your ears alert.

Radio Sheffield folk are natural wordsmiths and I've heard Southerner Dean Pepall use *'mi ol''* addressing Katie. An example of the power of local words to impress newcomers.

Note when I say 'pure Sheffield'. I can't say for sure that a word or phrase is not used elsewhere. My nephew David Poole - a bloke blessed with a keen ear - went to see his team, Brighton and Hove Albion (nobody's perfect) play at Pride Park

Stadium, Derby. A Derby fan urged on one of the attacking Rams
"Come on mi ol' ".

I was lucky enough to go with metallurgist Roy H. on several joint sales/metallurgical visits to factories that bought Rotherham steel (and probably still do) in Sweden, Norway, Denmark, France and Germany.

Roy made no concessions and spoke with the same Rotherham accent whether addressing managing director or sweeper-up, Frenchman, German or Scandinavian. A Danish garden tool factory, Zincks Fabbriker, were experiencing cracking with our steel when hot forging spades, after years of successful production. Roy found they were now working at too high a temperature, hence the cracks. *"Continue like that and tha'rt in dead lumber"*, he said to their heat treatment manager, and the Dane understood!

Driving us past lakes and through miles of forest towards customers in Mora, Sweden, our Swedish agent said *"Well, Roy, how do you like Sweden?"*

"It's all woods and watter" said Roy, puffing on his fag.

Roy told me a nice tale about the Brinsworth Cold Rolling Mill worker who had cheese sandwiches every day. *"Cheyse ageean. Cheyse ageean"*, the worker would say when opening his snap tin. Eventually Roy said *"Why dunt tha get thi missis ter mek thi summat else?"*

"What's tha meean?", said the worker, *"I mek 'em missen"*.

A friend of mine, Brian Hall, interested in dialect, told me old Sheffielders in engineering works used to say *'sam 'od'* - get hold: *'sam 'od will tha'*. Brian did German at Firth Park and thinks it stems from the German *sammeln* - to gather, collect. (The Hallamshire Glossary, 1828, though, has *sam*, to collect together - Anglo Saxon *samen*).

Brian formed a charitable football club in Dronfield in aid of severely disabled children and they played in monks' garb (Hope they never *'got 'monk on'* when they were playing - acted mardily). They called themselves the 'Muck or Nettles' (monc) club (=last ditch effort, *'all or nowt'* tackle). If anyone got too big for their boots - or habits - they'd be called the *'cock o' midden'* (dung heap). Brian's wife, June, adds if habits were torn and not stitched up correctly, the cloth is "snurled up" = creased or crumpled.

Chapter Nine - Local Words (recognisable nationally)

Many 'Sheffield' words are of course merely 'national' words spoken with a Sheffield accent. I list some - not in any order (I don't want to make it too easy for you).

Nooase: nose.

Clooers: clothes. My dad used to say he could sleep on a *clooers* line. I thought this was a silly expression until I heard that men at the tramps hostel on West Bar (tram conductors would call out *"Chatsworth House!"* when stopping there) used to sleep standing up with arms slumped over a rope - the cheapest nightly rest!

Clooers 'orse: clothes horse, also known as a *'winter(h)edge'*.

Oyal: hole.

Coyal: coal.

Coyal oyal: coal house.

Chip oyal: chip shop (never *fish oyal* - and never *'chippie'*) sometimes *chip og*.

Cake oyal: mouth.

Tony Capstick, a few weeks ago on Radio Sheffield, raised the conundrum *"If oyal is hole, what is oil?"* Answer: *"greease!"*

Fon: found. *'He looks like he's lost a bob an' fon a tanner'*.

Loise: lose.

Key: this is pronounced like *weigh*.

Keyse: keys. *'He's allus loisin' his keyse'*.

Peyse: peas. *'Skoyal peyse are like mabs* (marbles)*'.*

Cheyse: cheese.

Wiart: unless.

Not wiart: not unless.

*Nine **while** five:* until. Common with young and old. I'm sure the story is apocryphal that a Sheffielder died on a level crossing after reading the warning DO NOT CROSS WHILE LIGHT IS RED. We're not that daft, are we?

Teeam: team.

Creeam: cream.

Afooer: before. My Heeley friend Jack's 'mam' used to say *"ah've 'eard ducks fart afooer"* when she thought he was trying it on with her.

Dooer: door.

Flooer: floor. *"They're settin' women on on 'flooer"* (2001 broadcast about Don Valley steelworks - women working in Templeborough rolling mills - on the shop floor - during the war - *workin' wi' tongs*).

Mooer: more. *Mooer* is also, correctly, 'moor'. Doesn't it sound silly when Sheffielders, trying to be posh, talk about walking on the 'mores', and say 'more hen' instead of '*mooer* hen'.

Ooam: home. *'Ooz ee when eez at ooam?'*

Rooad: road. *'Any rooad up let's continue'*.

Corsey (causeway)*:* pavement. Causey, French *chaussee.*

Corsey edge: pavement edge.

This affs: this afternoon. *'Ah tha dooin' owt this affs?'* My French friend Michel and his mates used to say *'staprem'* (*cet après-midi*) - and Ozzies and Rony Robinson say *'this arvo'.* I was about to say "Shame on you, Rony", but Mary, my wife, likes this Ozzism - so I'll let thee off.

Neet is night. *'Sithee terneet'.*

Leet is light.

But *reet* is not 'right'. Mimics of our accent usually fall for this one. So in the magazine 'Old Bike Mart', April 1997, the review of Sheffield biker extraordinaire Wilf Green's autobiography, 'A Large Helping of Yorkshire Pudding', was headlined 'A REET RIPPING YARN!'

Reight is 'Right'. *'Orreight mi ol?'.*

Feight: fight. *'Wanna feight?'* Answer: *seven* (Infantile play on words - 'one off eight')

Meight: meat.

Eight: eat. As Fred Smith (from *dahn* Attercliffe) said after we'd been swimming at Hillsborough Baths, his nose pressed against a butcher's window: *"Ah could eight a meight pie!"* (Past tense and participle: *et, etten*).

43

A play on words by infant Neepsenders was:

*"I'll say **'I'll one a deead horse'**, you say **'I'll two a deead horse'** "* ….. etc …..
"Ah, tha says tha'll eight (eat) *a deead horse!"* Well, it seemed funny when you were seven or eight years old.

I was reminded of this childish joke when a bloke rang into Rony Robinson's Tell a Joke show recently on Radio Sheffield:

"Somebody was having their snap on 'Town Hall steps. What time was it by the Town Hall clock? *Summat to eight*" (something to eat).

All is not lost!

Watter: water. 'Brylcreem' hair oil came out after the war and those of us who couldn't afford it said we used 'corporation hair oil' - tap *watter*. (Sheffield Corporation ran the waterworks in those days).

Booan: bone.

Stooan: stone. A piece of *donkey stooan* (for whitening the step) was given to you by the Rag & Bone man in the 1940s in exchange for old rags.

Stooanses: Stones beer which used to be brewed in Neepsend. R.I.P.

Beer off: off licence shop.

Wesh: wash. Used by Chaucer in the 1300s. *Ah'm gunner mek thee an honorary Sheffielder, Geoffrey mi ol'.*

Babby: baby. When our Susan was two, she could whistle, and a woman said to her friend *"Ah've never 'eard a babby whistle afooer".*

Rooarin': crying (of baby). In Leeds they say *'roaring'*. I've heard Rony use it on

Radio Sheffield recently.

Mun: must.

Mont (pronounced as *won't*)*:* must not. *'Tha mont do that'* is quite a strong admonition.

Missen: myself.

Thissen: thyself.

Hersen: herself.

Hissen: himself.

Your sen: yourself.

Your sens: yourselves.

Us sens: ourselves.

Thersens: themselves.

But *onesen* is not 'oneself' because one never uses 'one' in Sheffield, does one - unless saying *'tha'rt a reight 'un, thee'* (you are a right one, you).

Yor lot: you lot.

Albert A. speaking to Séverine, a French woman working with us at Brinsworth Strip Mills about twenty years ago: *"If yor Froggies had listened to us there'd have been no French revolution!"* Straight John Bull was Albert! Séverine countered: *"Albert, vous êtes raciste!"*

Neow: no. There are two ways of saying 'no' in Sheffield dialect. One is a short,

45

sharp, no-nonsense *now* - pronounce the 'ow' as a Sheffielder pronounces *owd* (old), or *cowd* (cold), not as in 'cow'. The other is a longer, more dismissive *neow* (pronounced almost like a drawn-out Southern dipthonged English 'now').

Aah: yes.

Ooo aah: yes (more emphatic). My daughter Sue has a keen ear for language and once went to the wedding of a Sheffielder to a Devonian. She says half the guests were saying *'Ooo aah, ooo aah'*, the other half *'Ooo arrr, ooo arrr'*!

Ooer: over, or overtime. Sue once worked on the shop floor of Richardson's knife factory , and a genteel Sri Lankan lady who spoke impeccable English used to ask her in a lilt *"Are you working ooer?"* An example of newcomers learning the language.

'O' is added as a diminutive, or affectionate term. So Dean Pepall at Radio Sheffield becomes *'Deano'*, as did Brian Deane when at Bramall Lane. Coronation Street becomes *'Coro'* ('Corrie' elsewhere) and Wellington boots becomes *'Wellos'* ('Wellies' elsewhere).

Wain't: will not. *'God knows an' he wain't snitch'* (courtesy Hillfoot County Infants School, 1944-49). *'They wain't have it'* - said about today's youth who don't want to do physical work.

Gie: give. *'Gie it 'mester'* - a woman to her child ('Give it to the gentleman').

Gen: gave. *'He geniter'* ('He gave it to her').

'Eead: head. Reg Reid uses the word *'Pob 'eeads'* for youths who scribble on walls. (In our day the only graffiti you saw was communist slogans on the Five Arches, such as OPEN SECOND FRONT NOW and FREE THE ROSENBERGS). Reg is an ex Desert Rat - 'England's Bilko' - who asked if he could sign up again after the war and the Army replied *'Reid, the army can't afford you'*. Warning - I've promised to write Reg's story next.

Aif: half.

Deead: dead.

Aif deead: half dead. Doris W., who lives near the shop, remembers her mother Margery making armaments at Dormer Drills, Summerfield St., during the war, and coming home extremely tired.

"I'm aif deead", she said. Her dad corrected her: *"Margery - **half** deead!"*

Weer: where. *'Weer shalla purrit?'*

Theer: there. *'Purrit dahn theer, will tha.'*

Owt: anything.

Nowt: nothing. *'We sell nowt but Tools'* - sign in Ken Hawley's famous tool shop, 1950s-1990s.

Owt for nowt: what every Yorkshireman dreams of.

Summat for nowt: as above. *'Is summat up or summat?'*

Summat: free ad newspaper from Sheffield Newspapers, 2001.

Sidy (pronounced as 'tidy'): 'Sidy 'table'. Side the table, or clear the table. Not to be confused with:

Sidee ('sithee'): look. *'Sidee at this, sidee'.*

Er er mer er: filling-in sounds by children. I was surprised when a workman doing a job for us when we lived in Woodseats commenced each sentence with *'er er mer er'.*
The same bloke said *'ah 'a'* (*'ah 'at'* - like that). The ultimate in minimalism,

though I hope it isn't peculiar to Sheffield - otherwise we look reight ignorant, don't we?

Shufflin': I only heard this in the phrase *'Ah tha shufflin?'* - are you playing at dominoes? (Park Gate, 1960s).

Silent morn: This is the epithet thrown at someone who doesn't say much - who keeps his views to himself - who isn't open. (Heard 2001 from Malc M. - sounds as though it might be from an old hymn, 'Hail Silent Morn').

Mam: mother. In the sixth form at Firth Park Grammar School, I used to translate pop songs of the day into Sheffield dialect. I can only remember one - a song about the Bible: 'There's a book that my mother gave me'. Translation*: 'Dis a book what mi mam gen mi'.*
You know what I'm going to say......it seemed funny at the time!

Father is pronounced 'father' not 'farther'. To illustrate the conservativism of Sheffield Industry Wilfred Pickles told of the journeyman filemaker who carried a stout stick across his shoulders with a bag full of files on one end and a bag full of bricks on the other. *"Why don't you put files in both bags?"*, someone asked. The file maker replied *"What wor good enough for mi father's good enough for me"*.

Over the years I've heard words like *heighth* for height (matching width and breadth); *sempt* for seemed; *clomb* and *dove* for climbed and dived. These are more especially heard in Rotherham but they are probably national. *Clomb* and *dove* I think are American.

Ehen Alistair Lofthouse came to Sheffield from Cambridgeshire he was surprised to find "us" used to mean "my" as well as "our".

Gie it us: Give it to me.

We're gooin' on us own: We're going on our own.

Chapter Ten - Local Words (unrecognisable by national populace)

(Note again I'm not putting these in alphabetical order - that would be too easy for you. You might fall asleep reading them).

Slop dosh: the wet mud, usually in the gutter one played with as infants, damming the trickle of water.

Tiggy: childish game. If you were 'on' you tapped someone, and they were then on unless they shouted 'Kings' and froze - out of danger they would shout 'Queens' and run about again.

Hiddy: game of hiding. 'Coming, ready or not'.

I've hiddidit: I've hidden it. Note the *h* is always silent.

Icky: A boy's name used in the phrase *"Icky wi' his eye cut"*. = A mother's answer to an inquisitive child in answer to his persistent "who was that Mam?" This courtesy of Jacqui Reid (born on' Manor) and Mel Roberts (born on' Shirecliffe).

Leet is 'light', as we've said, but what about:

Lillilo: a word mothers would use to infants to mean (pretty) lights. They would also say *polly* for head, *danny* for hand and *tushy pegs* for teeth, but I believe these are known nationally.

Nesh: Claire Poole tells me this word is used in Stoke, and a Halifax bloke says they say *nash*. (We were talking to him on a cold day on a Victorian steamer on Lake Coniston a few years ago). The word is even in the dictionary - **'nesh'**, Old English HNESCE, unknown origin = susceptible to the cold. We know its origin, with its subtle shades of meaning, don't we? - the Steel City, of course.

Our Rachel gets called *nesh* at Wath College with the advice *"Tha wants to change thi butcher!"*

No self-respecting boy would wear gloves in winter down Neepsend -supposing he ever had any. If you did, someone would be sure to say *"th'art nesh, thee!"* To this day I can't wear gloves. If you didn't jump into the cold North sea at Life Boy camp in Staithes you were *nesh* - or you'd *neshed it.* You'd also *neshed it* if, when playing football, you didn't go in to tackle an opponent. Mono, who has done the cartoons for this book, says the term is still used in North Anston, but people are more likely to say you'd *'bottled out'.* (Where's the character in that, though?) While supporting United, I also enjoyed being on the Kop at Hillsborough (SPION KOP is painted today in blue and white paint above an entrance to the Kop end of the ground - you know of course this harks back to a battle in the Boer war in 1901). The Gates at Hillsborough were opened ten minutes before the end of the match and sometimes us kids went just for these last moments of the game for nowt.

I quietly absorbed the atmosphere, watching and listening to the fans as well as watching the play on the field. In the 1950s Wednesday had a centre half called Cyril Turton - 'Mother Turton', the fans called him, as he marshalled the players around him. He had the ability to run very fast backwards, elbows flailing to get back to his own half. He was a good player, well liked by the crowd, but one day he did this without challenging an opposing player who then ran round him and scored. A Wednesdayite in front of me turned to his mate - both in regulation flat caps - and said *"He's neshed it, sithee!"*

Here we have a rugby player 'neshing' a tackle. Can we blame him?

Baltic: very cold weather (Mexborough). There was a big trade with the Baltic states via the Sheffield and South Yorkshire Navigation.

Fair clemm'd: used if you were cold and *creddled* (cradled? = born) in Mexborough. (This courtesy of Nicky B). I've heard *clemm'd* before - perhaps a national word? Dave D (March 2002) says this is used also to mean very hungry. He reminds me that *starved* can mean very cold in Sheffield.

Mardy: someone who is spoilt, sullen, or won't join in. This word, more than **nesh**, is used by a broad swathe of the populace across the North Midlands and South Yorkshire. Like *nesh*, it is not heard north of Barnsley.

Walking on Kinder Scout recently I talked with a woman from Leek, Staffordshire, and she described her son as *mardy*. The word is common in D. H. Lawrence's North Notts. When we lived in Manchester we found they shortened the word to *mard*, and Claire in Stoke confirms *mard* is used there more there than *mardy*. On the other hand, I've heard *mardy* used in Manchester - based Coronation Street. Fred Elliott, 5/9/01, even used it as a noun - *"I don't want to be a mardy"*. Perhaps they've a South Yorkshire writer occasionally, because I've also heard Sheffield glottal stops.

Scutch: to cuff with the flat of the hand across the back of someone's head. Usually mother hitting an errant male child or teacher hitting a naughty boy. Policemen, too, handled minor infringements of the law by young lads by *scutching 'em*. Common in Barnsley, Mexborough, Sheffield. Mary's found in the 'English Duden' that *scutch* is a term used in the linen industry - and there was a linen industry in Barnsley.

Whittle: another Sheffield classic - to moan, to grumble, to go on and on worrying or *mithering* about something. A Sheffield word through the ages, both a verb and a noun. A trade term - originally a general, workaday knife. Chaucer, bless him, in the 1300s gave our fledgling cutlery industry a boost in the Reeve's Tale when he described the tough miller - he who could break any door down 'at a running with his heed' - as carrying a Sheffield knife in his stocking:

(Note the lack of the *'i'* in Sheffield - Sheffielders to this day talk of *'Sheffel'*.) The word *thwitel* - knife - has its echoes right down to the present day. There's a cheap knife still made called *whittle tang*; there's a *whittling knife* for paring wood and, of course, the verb *to whittle* means to shave a piece of wood down to shape, and, by extension, to pare down one's nerves as mentioned above.

Panshon: big bowl. Bread was 'sad' if it didn't rise in it.

Dolly Posh: old Sheffield dialect for left-handed, no doubt stemming from the dolly tub and wooden three-legged posher which I vaguely remember being wielded by brawny-armed women. Professor Widdowson of Sheffield University is an expert on Sheffield language and lore, and at a lecture he gave at the Trades Historical Society he asked the 30-strong audience what the Sheffield dialect was for left-handed. There were choruses of *'cack-handed'* - only little me gorrit reight: *Dolly Posh*. He said it's no longer used, but it is - albeit rarely. Quite popular in the 1940s and 50s. I've only heard it used on Ecclesall Road three or four times in the last eighteen years. Such hearings give great pleasure - like spotting a rare bird.

Sprottling: a favourite of mine, reported extinct - but I've heard it twice in my lifetime. If not like spotting the Dodo, it certainly equals sighting the Cornish Chough.

The word means moving around, thrashing around ineffectually (either physically or verbally); floundering. I first heard it from Harry Gill in around 1990. Harry, a plumber from Calver, splendid Derbyshire accent and mischievous sense of humour, raconteur, amusing digs at Sheffielders, the heathens over the hills. It was a pleasure to have him in the '475 club' (our shop).

Manchester United had been on the television and their big Danish goalkeeper had famously run around in his goal area - running out, running back, falling over, reaching his hands out vainly as the ball bounced into the net.

"What did you reckon o' Schmeichel", Harry said, *"sprottlin' about in 'goalmouth?"*

I next heard it in 2001 just after the Election. Malcolm M., a hand engraver of great skill, walking with me on Kinder said *"Hague hasn't got the image, but if you listen to what he actually says, he leaves Blair sprottlin"*. Magic! (Whether or not you agree with him politically).

Joan B. agrees the word is seldom heard now but remembers the phrase *What tha sprottlin' at?* - 'what are you struggling to do?' and the father's admonition of the gawky teenager *sprottled out* - sprawled out on the floor in everybody's way. So ironically it can also indicate a lack of animation. Dave D (March 202) quotes *"Look at 'im all spottled out in that sofa"*. Also a pricelass one quoted by a lady on Ecclesall Road: *"Sprottled out like lamb and lettuce!"* I'm told it's even used for a sound - if a motorbike is misfiring it's *"sprottling"*.

Siling it down: another little treasure: raining heavily. *To sile it down.* I've never heard it used in England apart from in Sheffield and district, but some areas of Scotland know it. A Norwegian lady came in our shop in May 2001 and she said *sile* was a Norwegian word meaning 'to rain like a foss (waterfall)'. Hunter (Hallamshire Glossary 1828) thinks it derives from the word sile, meaning a fine sieve through which milk was passed to free it from hairs and impurities.

Spice: Sheffield for sweets. Go and see Granelli's shop sign at the bottom of Broad St.: 'Old Fashioned Spice at an Old Fashioned Price'. Eccellente!

Brummies call spice *rocks*. I know this because as youngsters we went youth hostelling at Castleton and met with some Brummies. They thought we were talking about herbs, we thought they were referring to fossils in Cave Dale. *"Language **is** a barrier"*, as my mother once famously said to my French pen pal. Michel, puzzled and not understanding a word, eventually came out with *"Yes. Byron is a very nice boy!"*

Byron was (and is) my cousin - then a miner at Manton Colliery - who impressed Michel with his politeness to other road users when he drove us around Derbyshire. Michel's English wasn't good, but when Byron and his friends thee'd and thou'd together and greeted people with *"Orreight mi ol' luv"* he was flummoxed. *"Are they speaking English?"* he once asked me.

Byron's one who always speaks his mind and occasionally it costs him his job. Working as a plumber after his stint down the mine he was called to a top floor flat up Fulwood. He mended a leak and was heading downstairs when the lady in the flat below called him in. "What are you going to do about this?" she asked, pointing at her ceiling light in its glass bowl - half full of water. *"If I wor thee luv, I'd put a couple o' goldfish in it"* was his parting reply.

He worked with Thomas Craig (stage name Craig Thomas - red haired Sheffielder in 'Where the Heart Is' TV series). He saw him in an amateur production of 'West Side Story' and was immensely impressed. So much so that he told Thomas *"tha wants to tek up acting......'cos tha'rt a crap plumber!"*

Spogs: a Mexborough alternative to *spice*.

Shunkley: shiny dress- reported by Tony Capstick on Radio Sheffield, April 2001. I'd never heard of it before - may be local to Mexborough?

Snurped up: turned up, wrinkled up of cloth, stitching.

Scrome: *scroming about* - walking, climbing awkwardly, e.g. up the rocks at Grindsbrook.

Slair: *slairing* - sliding with your hob-nailed boots.

Shant: pronounced as 'ant'. Only used in the phrase *'All o'er 'shant'* (all over the place). *'Her clooers are all o'er 'shant.'*

Sneck: door latch.

Badly: feeling ill, feeling poorly, feeling *off 'hooks*. I've heard *'took badly'* in 'Coro' (Coronation Street).

Kale: turn, place in a queue.

Get in thi kale = 'take your turn in the queue'.
I'll loise mi kale = 'I'll lose my turn'.
I'm out o' mi kale
It's my kale (Hallamshire Glossary 1828)

Bill Hukin, razor grinder, once said he supposed someone had *kale'd* him (when his NHS eye operation was delayed).

Jennel: pathway, passageway by and/or through buildings widely used - often seen in 'The Star' newspaper. Sometimes (in error I think) used nowadays for the passageway through terraced houses to gain access to the back yard. We always knew this as the *entry*. *"Go and play in yer own entry"* was the cry if we played cricket down someone's 'entry', batsman holding a piece of wood, defending stumps drawn in chalk on a bin!

Leeds folk and others say *ginnel* ('g' as in grin, not gin).
While mentioning Leeds folk I must pay them tribute for a gem of a word:

Thoil: used by Mary's Aunty Daisy for someone who couldn't bear to part with his money. *"He can't thoil to spend aught"*, she'd say, eyes darting about, both malicious and funny. She also used it in a more positive sense to mean endure - *'he'd thoil anything for his boys'*. In this connection you must read Rabbie Burns' poem ***'To a Mouse** (on turning her up in her nest with the plough, November 1785)'*:

..That wee bit heap o' leaves an' stibble,
Has cost thee monie a weary nibble!
Now thou's turned out, for a' thy trouble,
....
*To **thole** the winter's sleety dribble,*
....

(The little mouse turned out of its nest to **endure** the winter). Note how Burns uses the familiar form *thee* and *thou* to address the *'wee sleekit, cowrin', tim'rous beastie'*.

Black bright: very dirty. Paul Iseard got this expression from Nicky B.'s list of Mexborough words. From coalmining, where the coal on the miners' faces would glint in the sun as they came off their shift , before the days of pithead baths. Mary remembers the phrase from her childhood in Leeds where she lived in sight of a pit.

Frame thissen: 'Get a grip of yourself' (army), 'take charge of yourself' (navy). Used in Sheffield but more in Leeds, probably a national, if little used, phrase - as in 'now you're framing'.

Chuff: *Chuffed* nationally means pleased, but to be called a *chuff* in Sheffield is to be mildly sworn at, to be mildly insulted - although a woman called me a *'reight chuff'* recently and she sounded quite affectionate!

Ken Hawley is a down to earth Sheffielder whose world-renowned collection of Sheffield tools ought to be housed in the city's Millennium galleries - with part toured around the country. I once asked him why he objected to a certain person. *"Because he's a chuff"* was his immediate and only reply.

As a young man I used to listen to people and say nowt. Now I'm afraid I rattle on a lot and once, when I'd arranged for Ken to record an ex-buffer girl on tape, he got exasperated with me butting in and said "Shurrup chuff, an' tha'll learn summat". I wasn't insulted. (I would have been if he'd called me a **gormless** chuff!)

My friend Reg Reid described someone as a *reight braungin' chuff* (*braungin'* = bragging).

A much milder expletive than *effin' 'ell* is *chuffin' 'ell*. There is a group of Sheffield women with the inspired name of **Chuffinelles**!

Crozzle: you couldn't get more local than this - it should be in the Trades section but I thought it deserved a 'pog' among the Sheffield classics.

Crozzle is the waste slag from the old conical cementation furnaces that made the celebrated 'shear' steel. Look for old Sheffield knives marked 'shear' or 'double shear' steel and you will find on sharpening that they have a vicious edge! (One of the furnaces is still preserved at Hoyle St., Sheffield, and I believe it was producing shear steel for Daniel Doncasters right up to 1951).

The slag, when broken, was black, glassy and sharp, and chunks were much used on tops of walls to deter little lads from climbing over. You can still see *crozzle* topping walls all along the riversides - and in localities all over Sheffield. There are sightings at the top end of Norfolk Park and on the high wall at Arnold Laver's old woodyard on Queens Road. There are soon to be new developments on this last site, and I think we ought to organise a *'Save our Crozzle'* campaign!

By extension, the word *crozzled* is used to describe bacon, crisp and burnt black at the edges.

Puthering: used of smoke billowing out. Very rarely heard now with clean steelmaking, and with the demise of coal fires, their smoke *puthering* out to the skies through their 'chimbley pots'.

Snided (with): full of - an excellent word. When dialect words fill a niche, they survive - and *snided* is such a word. It is often heard on Radio Sheffield:

- In March 2001 a Maltby lady rang their gardening programme for help. She said last year her apple tree was *snided* with woolly aphids.
- In the same month Rony Robinson introducing Dr Rose McNaughton urged listeners to *'snide her out with questions'*.
- John Clarke, Sheffield knife collector extraordinaire, London born, Sheffield bred, talked of Ecclesall Road and London Road *'snided with traffic'*.
- The saddest use was a comment by my sister Mary after breast surgery, when we were trusting that her cancer had been conquered: *"Perhaps I'm snided wi' it"*. She was.

Tranklements: bits and pieces, ornaments.

Surrey, serri, (sirrah?): another favourite of mine, though I've never heard it used in Sheffield. I mentioned earlier that my mother's dad, George Hopkinson ex Matlock, Derbyshire, addressed people as *surrey* (this would be 1910 to ca. 1930).

In D. H. Lawrence's novels, 'Sons and Lovers', 'Lady Chatterley's Lover', etc. covering North Notts to the south of Sheffield, some characters make much use of this form of address.

Malc D., my boss at Brinsworth Strip Mills, Rotherham, was 'Welsh by extraction, Scotch by absorption' (his words). His dad, a miner, had walked from South Wales to seek work in the Nottinghamshire coal mines during the depression of the 1930s. He found work at Creswell Colliery, and in the 1950s he went on a miners' coach trip to London. It may have been after the Cresswell pit disaster. They were treated to a meal at a posh restaurant. A waiter came round with jugs of coffee and of cream and asked a young miner if he wanted black or white coffee. The miner looked puzzled. He'd never heard of white coffee before so ordered black. The waiter poured the coffee and walked away. *"Ey up surrey"* the miner bellowed after him *"Tha's put no milk in this!"* Priceless!

Paul Iseard, who took over **the Sheffield Shop** on 'Ecks Rooad' in September 2001 and who has Mexborough connections says *serri* is used there to address a person you don't know or whose name you can't remember.

Addressing man to man there are countless words: ***jarv*** (Mexborough again); ***youth*** (North Notts); ***boss*** (Army 1960s); and, of course, ***mi ol'***. Fred Mansfield, who ran the Woodseats School of Motoring, addressed his male pupils as ***captain***. When I suggested I had priority at a roundabout he said *"Famous last words, captain"*.

'Udge up! or ***Budge up!:*** move up, please.

Like burkses: to move fast. (I heard this in Rotherham - Thrybergh to be exact!)

A Brussen bloke: a nasty, horrible bloke (in Mexborough and Barnsley). Mary B. says this was used in Sheffield for a small, stocky bloke - not necessarily a nasty one!

Bonny: pretty in the rest of the country, but in Sheffield pleasantly plump. Hunter's 'Hallamshire Glossary' gives: 'in good health….handsome, as applied to a young girl'.

In Hunter's time and in my youth to be healthy was to have a bit of weight on you. One of the steelworkers at Andrews Toledo, Neepsend, wide leather belt slung under his massive beer belly, saw skinny little me being barged aside in a football game and came out with the comment: "tha wants to get some puddin' dahn thi".

Mashing: you all know this - making tea (brewing in the South), but I'm told mashing in Barnsley can mean snogging, as does:

Mankin': boy playing around with girl or vice versa.

Capertling: according to Mike B., 2001, is flirting, on the way to *mankin'*.

Manky: lairy, loppy, not very good. (Not to be confused with *mankin'*)

Yitten: frightened. Me, Alan Cottingham, Bob Simpson and a few others were in Brian Simpson's gang. This was before we joined the Life Boys at the instigation of my mother who thought young boys had to be guided or they got into trouble. We did nothing wrong in Brian's gang - only some things that were quite dangerous, like running - or in my case walking gingerly - on the big gas pipe that ran from one part of the gasworks high above Parkwood Road into another part. If you didn't do it there was a danger someone might say *"th'art yitten!"* This word was locked away at the back of my mind, then I heard Ian Macmillan, the Barnsley bard, quote *'th'art yitten'* on Radio Sheffield recently.

Wazzock: an idiot.

Closet: a *wazzock* or toilet

Wazz: (rude) to pee.

Bobar: (childish) to do a poo.

Dodo: child's dummy.

Chapter Eleven - Some Key Expressions

A stranger to Sheffield thought that two women he overheard were Chinese.

One said *"Oowashiwee? Washiwee'ersen?"*

The other replied *"Shewowee'ersen"*.

They were, of course, saying:

"Who was she with? Was she on her own?"

"She was on her own".

In the sixth form at Firth Park Grammar School 1954-55 lists of Sheffield dialect phrases were passed around - rather like illicit religious texts in Communist Russia! The lists were passed from school to school - origin unknown. I re-typed these in the form of a quiz and have still got a copy forty-seven years on. The fact that I mentioned East Grinstead shows the influence of the Goon show at the time.

Here goes:

English as spoke on 'Wicker (weer t'watter runs o'er t'weer), or:

SHEFFIELD IN THE RAW.

SHEFFIELD - ENGLISH LANGUAGE TEST. Time allowed: 20 minutes.

10 correct answers:- you are an immigrant from East Grinstead.

25 correct:- you're on the way to being a settler.

40 correct:- you're from Rotherham.

All correct:- it's time you brushed up your Queen's English.

Translate to English: (N.B. The 'g' is hard - as in 'got').

1. Intitot.
2. Giuzit.
3. Summatsupeer.
4. Gerritetten.

5. Gerartnit.
6. Supwidee?
7. Smarrerweeim?
8. Iampgorrit.
9. Azee geniter?
10. Geeitmester.
11. Eez gooinooam.
12. Astha gorrit withy?
13. Eesneshedit sithee.
14. Atha splodgin'?.
15. Purrimineer.
16. Aberra lerra gooan gerrit ersen.
17. Thalafter gerra newun.
18. Eesezitintiz burraberritiz.
19. Lerrus gerrus andswesht.
20. Sumonemz gorragerroff.
21. Atha dooin owt terneet?
22. Thamun gerrit lernt.
23. Shut thigob.
24. Ahzeeno?
25. Cantha kumtahrowse terneet?
26. Aberritinterz.
27. Nardendee, wotdardooin?
28. Supwidee? / Supwithee?
29. Corforus aifpasteight in 'morning.
30. It dunt marrer.
31. Tintintin sithee.
32. Asthagorratanner?
33. Eenose nowt abartit.
34. Eez gunna gerra lorra lolly forrit.
35. Lerra gerron 'bus.
36. Eedurnt purrizeead under 'watter.
37. Eesezeeantaddit.
38. Ooworriwee? Worriweeissen?

39. Ateldim burriwunt lissen.

40. Lerrim purrizaton.

41. Assel clout thee iftha dunt geeooar.

42. Is summat up or summat?

43. Gerrary tergithi andweeit.

44. Eez gorrizatooam.

45. Tha wantster wesh thi eeroils aht.

46. Get thissen off ooam. Gerroff ooam.

47. Thakan if tha wants.

48. Eez nobbut a babbi.

49. Get thi cooat on, wi gooin ooam.

50. Weers gaffer?

Answers:

1. Isn't it hot?

2. Give it to me.

3. Something's amiss.

4. Please eat your food.

5. Please go away.

6. What's up with you?

7. What's the matter with him?

8. I haven't got it.

9. Has he given it to her?

10. Give it to the gentleman.

11. He's going home.

12. Have you got it with you?

13. He bottled out, look!

14. Are you going fishing?.

15. Put him in here.

16. I'd better let her go and get it herself.

17. You'll have to get a new one.

18. He says it isn't his, but I bet it is.

19. Let's go and wash our hands.

20. Some of them will have to get off.

21. Are you doing anything tonight?

22. You must learn it.

23. Please be quiet.

24. How does he know?

25. Can you come to our house tonight?

26. I bet it isn't hers.

27. Now then you, what are you doing?

28. What's up with you?

29. Call for me at half past eight in the morning.

30. It doesn't matter.

31. It isn't in the tin, look.

32. Have you got a tanner? (sixpence)

33. He doesn't know anything about it.

34. He's going to be well paid for it.

35. Let her get on the bus.

36. He daren't put his head under the water.

37. He says he hasn't had it.

38. Who was he with? Was he on his own?

39. I told him, but he wouldn't listen.

40. Let him put his hat on.

41. I shall hit you if you don't stop.

42. Is there something amiss?

43. Ask Harry if he will help you.

44. He's got his at home.

45. You need to listen more carefully.

46. Go home.

47. You can if you want to.

48. He's only a baby.

49. Put your coat on, we're going home.

50. Where is the boss?

In 1981 phrases such as these were included in the gem of a book 'Sheffieldish, a beginners phrase book', by Derek Whomersley, illustrations by Whitworth. It was published by the City of Sheffield Publicity Dept. and printed by Northends in Sheffield.

I had countless requests for this book since I opened the Sheffield Shop on Ecclesall Road in 1983 and I had to tell everybody *"it selt aht"*.

So *' if tha wants owt dooin, do it thissen'*. I eventually decided to write these my reflections on the language in 2001, the year I handed the shop over to Paul Iseard. Paul's not a native so it may be useful for him to chant these phrases like a mantra so he knows them by heart.

We like to think of ourselves as unique in Sheffield, like an engineering 'one off' - but I heard a lot of these same phrases - *tintintin*, *wotsupwithee* plus *laikin'* on a programme from a Barnsley junior school on Radio Sheffield in February 2001.

And I'm sure other cities such as Liverpool, Newcastle, London and Glasgow have similar lists with their rich local dialect and lore (nearly as rich as ours).

Glasgow and Sheffield have much in common - the great Sheffield steelman John Brown built ships on the Clyde, including the 'Queens' liners. We both suffered drastic cutbacks in Heavy Industry in the 1980s. We both have a posh West End and a working class East End. - And we've both been insulted by the Duke of Edinburgh! (When in Malaya he spoke with students hoping to study in Britain: "I don't know what you'll think of cities like Sheffield and Glasgow").

The Glasgow comedian Stanley Baxter did a nice skit on the language programmes popular in the 1970s. The scene was a market stall:

'Parliamo Glasgieano'
'Is there a marra on the barra, Clarra?'
etc. etc.

Chapter Twelve - Will the Sheffield Dialect Survive?

Who knows - but my instinct tells me it will. Its death has been forecast since Victorian times with the coming of the Railways.....

Today as well as levelling of language by radio and television, there's computer and text message speak.

There's American influence of course: 'fill out', 'next up', 'listen up', 'schedule' (*skedule* for *shedule*), 'downsize', adopted by breathless TV presenters and DJs.

There's Liverpudlian influence - probably from 'Brookie' (Brookside) and Scouse football managers:

'stupid' becomes *shtupid*
'student' becomes *shtudent* etc.
I've heard *purshue* and even *ashbestiosis* by Radio Sheffield presenters.

There's Cockney influence - perhaps from DJs and 'East Enders':

'drawing' becomes *droring*
'water' becomes *wa'er* (the Cockney mid-glottal stop as mentioned earlier)
'thing' and 'through' become *fing* and *froo*.

On BBC Radio Sheffield 'Praise or Grumble' in March 2001 speaking about Sheffield Wednesday's recovery under Peter Shreeves (himself an arch-Cockney, bless him!) a Sheffield lad with otherwise impeccable Sheffield dialect ended *"results are cumin' froo nah"*.

Though to my surprise, *What's the damage?* (how much?) *Chuck* (term of endearment) and *Fall* (autumn) which I thought were Cockney/Lancashire/American respectively, all appear in 'The Hallamshire Glossary'!

There's Ozzie slang and Ozzie intonation which makes every statement a question. There must be a name for it in linguistics but I'm sure you'll be aware of what I mean.

Even in the TV series 'Heartbeat', which is supposedly set in 1960s North Yorkshire, this Ozzie querulous intonation is in evidence. Perhaps she was hiding something? (28/1/01). 'Heartbeat', in fact, shows those who lived in the 1960s how language continually develops. The programme has attention to detail with scenery and clothing, cars, buses, music, 'street furniture' all faithful to the 1960s. But apart from Claud Greengrass (Bill Maynard) , all the characters speak 1990s English:

Sorry? for 'pardon?' 'eh?' or 'tha what?'
Absolutely for 'yes'
The barmaid says *"there you go"* for 'there you are'.

And, inexcusably, they mention the Swiss Army Knife instead of the stronger, no-gimmicks **British Army** Sheffield-made knife which has seen more service in more countries than the Swiss Army - begging its pardon - have had hot dinners.

There's media/social services/business jargon such as 'empower', 'focused', 'outreach', 'input', 'learning curve', 'proactive', 'ring fence'. Nouns are used as verbs such as someone 'guesting' on a programme, and 'accessing' information. Of course there's 'resources' for money - even 'human resources' for people. One almost longs for those days when Lancastrian NUM president Joe Gormley used to demand 'cash on the table'.

There are filling in phrases:

'To be honest'
'You know what I'm saying'
'You know what I mean'

I was pleased to hear this last translated into Sheffield dialect from someone ringing Radio Sheffield: *"tha knows worrah meean Rony?"* - though I was hoping

Rony would reply *"Course ah know wot tha meeans. Does tha think ah'm daft or summat?"*

Where dialect words and phrases fill a gap or are amusing they will survive better than a lot of modern jargon, and newcomers throughout the years aren't necessarily immune to the charms of our dialect. I've mentioned the Sri Lankan lady saying *working ooer* and Londoner Dean Pepall at Radio Sheffield addressing Katie Galbraith as *mi ol'*.

When I was sixteen and seventeen in the 1950s I took summer school holidays on the railways as a porter at Midland Station and carriage cleaning at Heeley Sidings. At Heeley there were Jamaicans and Trinidadians only recently arrived in Britain, and they adopted Sheffield dialect quite quickly.

'Big Donald' (guess who was 'Little Donald'?), a six and a half foot Jamaican, would greet you with *"Now den dee, 'ow da gooin'? "* He came to work in a black trilby which he called *'my Hanthony Heden, man'* (the old school Anthony Eden was PM at the time). One morning I was asked to find him. He'd been seen to arrive but hadn't been seen since.

I found him in the broom cabin, sighting first his 'wellos' (Wellington boots - we don't say 'wellies') poking out from under mounds of cloths, towels, buckets, brushes and brooms. I pulled at them and an angry voice growled *"Leeave mi alooan - I was on de rug all last neet man"* - and, when I persisted, *"Ahs'll make a mess o' dee man!"*

Incidentally, all the West Indians said *ax* instead of 'ask', and I was surprised to read recently the following in Hunter's 'Hallamshire Glossary' (written about 170 years ago): *'Ax. To ask. Here the antient form is preserved by the common people'*. A case of - to use to-day's jargon - 'What goes around comes around'.

A final word from Mr Sangenvogeln from Youngstown, USA, who said the view from Wincobank Hill at Forgemasters in the Don Valley, Sheffield, looked for all the world like the view he used to see at Youngstown looking down at the big brooding sheds of US Steel. He married a Barnsley girl whose dad, a kindly ex-miner, baffled him at first: *"Sit thissen dahn mi old love - mek thissen at ooam"*. The American man made a very creditable attempt at the Sheffield dialect - (as did Ian Wright (ex Arsenal) when he interviewed Sheffield's Prince Naseem on TV).

I'll end with the goodbye that my youngest daughter Lucy now leaves me with:

"I'll sithee, surrey".

Addenda

Mr Roy Bullen has kindly lent me notes on our local language and lore which he copied for posterity to the University of Sheffield Centre for English Cultural Tradition and Language.

I list below some words and phrases that I find of interest or which amplify or clarify what I've written.

If children wanted to play at *Hiddy* or *Tiggy* and someone had to be chosen to be 'on', you could 'dip for it' - everyone would stand round with fists held out and someone would touch each fist while saying:

One potater
Two potater
Three potater four
Five potater
Six potater
Seven potater more.
One, Two, Three
Out goes THEE! ... etc.

If boys wanted to decide which cricket team would bat first and no coin was available (often the case!) the captains would *wet for it*. One would cup his hands

70

over his mouth, turn away and spit on one palm. He'd then turn palms down and the other had to guess which palm was wet.

If the ball was batted high into the long grass (or over the gasworks wall) it was *six and out*.

When there was a dispute in cricket the batsman had to run two runs whether he hit the ball or not: *Hit or miss, run two*.

After using up so much energy the boy might be accused back home of *golloping* his food (eating too fast), and he would be urged to *eat like a Christian*: don't 'gollop' your food.

I'm going off at a tangent here but at Park Gate Iron and Steel in the 1960s a biro was provided and when this ran out you had to take it to the Purchasing Department as proof, whereupon you were given another. I once went without proof and the clerk asked his boss, Tom Badger, if I could have a new one. *"Orreight"*, said Tom, *"- he's a Christian!"*

Lug oyal: ear. *Tha wants to wesh thi lug oyals aht.*

Six foot and a gaslamp: a tall fellow. (Or, vulgarly in Neepsend: *a long streak o' donkey snot*).

Snot rag: handkerchief.

You little **divil**: for devil. Mary's Aunty Daisy in Leeds also said *divil* . She used the word *scopperel* - in 'running about like a *scopperel*'. It sounds like an insect but I don't think it's a 'black clock' (beetle) which caused concern if spotted 'legging it' (to-day's jargon) towards the skirting board. *Scopperel* may be connected with Roy Bullen's *scoppodile* - overactive child.

Mi belly thinks mi throoat's cut: My mother also used this phrase which she got from her brother, Charlie, who would walk home 'black bright' from Thorncliffe

Colliery and have a bath in front of the fire before he could get his dinner. Classic working class stuff! My mother would wash his bruised and cut back. No wonder he was hungry. Famished. (This last also means 'cold' in Sheffield).

Throng: very busy.

Physog: face.

Put 'wood in 'oyal!: shut that door!

Shunkle: to shine (as in cheap jewellery). Cf. Tony Capstick speaking of a woman in a *shunkley* dress.

Nah then ahr kid: how are you?

Fair to middlin': so - so. In wide use - certainly as far south as Sewstern, near Grantham.

When I worked at Brinsworth Strip Mills we were linked up for a while with Whithead's Strip Mills at Newport. If I asked my opposite number down there how he was, he'd invariably reply *'Fair to mis-er-ab-le'*, in his precise Welsh accent.

Chaiteead: daft person.

Tha'rt as soft as Sheffield watter

Tha'rt as sharp as ahr double shear steel - 1903 Walker and Hall booklet. Obsolete steel making process but, as I've said before, look out for Victorian Sheffield shear steel knives. Watch your fingers!

The Crucible steel process - the world's first proper cast steel made on a commercial basis - invented in Sheffield in 1742 by Benjamin Huntsman - is also obsolete. You can see a 1950s pot from the Huntsman works in the Don Alexander Sheffield Shop. I mention this because to-day (18/10/01) I've had the pleasure of meeting Brian Hall in the Red Lion at Litton - ex landlord of the Black Bull, Foolow - ex production director at Jewel Blade - and way back in the 50s, as a lad, a *slagger-off* in Turners Crucible melting shop on Mowbray Street.

Shop floor talk - sometimes rude, sometimes gossip. Don Williams used to tell me how one man at Metros (Metropolitan Vickers, Attercliffe Common) would signal his friend, leave his machine, and they would be huddled in conversation = gossip. The rest of the men in the workshop would stay at their machines but sing in unison the rousing hymn:

'Tell me the old old story
Tell me the old old story….'

He's got all his chairs at home: is a lot nicer thing to say about a bloke than 'He's got a slate loose'.

Over to Leeds again. Daisy used to say *'She's got all her buttons on'* = sharp, not easily hoodwinked.

Eyes: or as heard in Rotherham market *'Nipples, stickin' aht like chapel 'at pegs.'*

Addenda over - I hope I haven't 'sounded off' in too pretentious a manner, because, in Roy's Walkley/Crookes childhood, lads would counter this sarcastically by *saying* *'True O King. May you live forever.'*

Be that as it may, as they say in Crookes/Walkley, and used to say in Halton, Leeds (Mary's stepmother, Vera), ***'Them as lives longest 'll see most'***.